AMERICAN ASSOCIATION OF
LEGAL NURSE CONSULTANTS

MW01063687

AMERICAN NURSES
ASSOCIATION

LEGAL NURSE CONSULTING:
SCOPE AND STANDARDS
OF PRACTICE

nurses
books
.org

The Publishing Program of ANA

AMERICAN NURSES ASSOCIATION
SILVER SPRING, MARYLAND

Library of Congress Cataloging-in-Publication data

American Association of Legal Nurse Consultants.
  Legal nurse consulting : scope and standards of practice / American Association of Legal Nurse Consultants.
     p. ; cm.
  Includes bibliographical references and index.
  ISBN-13: 978-1-55810-231-6 (pbk.)
  ISBN-10: 1-55810-231-0 (pbk.)
     1. Nursing consultants—Legal status, laws, etc.   2. Nursing—Law and legislation.
  3. Forensic nursing.   I. American Nurses Association.   II. Title.
     [DNLM: 1. Forensic Medicine—standards—United States—Guideline.
  2. Specialties, Nursing—standards—United States—Guideline.   3. Consultants—
  United States—Guideline.   4. Professional Practice—standards—United States—
  Guideline. WY 101 A512L 2006]

  RT73.L44 2006
  610.73—dc22   2006016278

The American Nurses Association (ANA) is a national professional association. This ANA publication—*Legal Nurse Consulting: Scope and Standards of Practice*—reflects the thinking of the nursing profession on various issues and should be reviewed in conjunction with state board of nursing policies and practices. State law, rules, and regulations govern the practice of nursing, while *Legal Nurse Consulting: Scope and Standards of Practice* guides nurses in the application of their professional skills and responsibilities.

Published by nursesbooks.org
The Publishing Program of ANA

American Nurses Association
8515 Georgia Avenue, Suite 400
Silver Spring, MD 20910
1-800-274-4ANA
http://www.nursingworld.org/

ANA is the only full-service professional organization representing the nation's 2.7 million Registered Nurses through its 54 constituent member associations. ANA advances the nursing profession by fostering high standards of nursing practice, promoting the economic and general welfare of nurses in the workplace, projecting a positive and realistic view of nursing, and lobbying the Congress and regulatory agencies on healthcare issues affecting nurses and the public.

The American Association of Legal Nurse Consultants (AALNC) is dedicated to the advancement and the professional enhancement and growth of Registered Nurses practicing in the specialty of legal nurse consulting (LNC). AALNC is the preeminent resource for professionals with an interest in the LNC arena including novice and veteran legal nurse consultants. AALNC provides networking opportunities, educational advancement, and professional development.

Design: Scott Bell, Freedom by Design ~ *Composition:* House of Equations, Inc. ~ *Copyediting:* Elizabeth M. Anthony ~ *Proofreading & indexing:* Steven A. Jent ~ *Printing:* McArdle Printing

First printing June 2006.

ISBN-13: 1-55810-231-0   ISBN-10: 978-1-55810-231-6   06SSLNC   2.5M   06/06

Contributors

Work Group Members

Karen A. Ballard, MA, RN, Chairperson
Karen Clark, MS, RN
Mindy Cohen, MSN, RN, LNCC
Barbara J. Levin, BSN, RN, ONC, LNCC
Jane Mihalich, BSN, RN, LNCC
Kammie Monarch, RN, JD

ANA Staff

Carol J. Bickford, PhD, RN, BC
Winifred Carson-Smith, JD
Yvonne Daley Humes, MSA

Dedication

To Legal Nurse Consultants who, in all their diverse practices, facilitate the interface between nursing, medicine, and the law with the ultimate goal of improving patient care and safety for all.

CONTENTS

INTRODUCTION

Legal Nurse Consulting: Scope and Standards of Practice outlines the expectations of the professional role in which all registered legal nurse consultants should practice. This scope statement and these updated standards of legal nurse consulting practice are meant to guide, define, and direct legal nurse consultant practice in all settings.

In 1995 the American Association of Legal Nurse Consultants (AALNC) developed the first legal nurse consultant standards of practice. In 2003 AALNC recognized the need to review and update the specialty scope and standards of practice to reflect the evolving practice of the legal nurse consultant, work that was published in *Legal Nurse Consulting: Principles and Practices* in 2003. A task force was established in 2004 to investigate recognition as a specialty nursing practice and further expand the standards on the model of the newly published American Nurses Association (ANA) *Nursing: Scope and Standards of Practice* (2004).

ANA has promoted development of statements of scope of practice and standards of practice since the late 1960s. It published the first *Standards of Nursing Practice* for the nursing profession in 1973. These standards were generic in nature and focused on the basic nursing process, a critical thinking model applicable to all registered nurses. The stages of the nursing process are assessment, diagnosis, outcomes identification, planning, implementation, and evaluation. Over the years various revisions have ensued. Specialty nursing organizations have affirmed this work by using the template language of the standards to develop scope of practice statements and standards of practice for registered nurses engaged in specialty practice.

By 2005, the AALNC Workgroup had begun work in earnest on this important endeavor. They met regularly to review and revise the specialty scope and standards, working in conjunction with ANA staff and others. ANA publications, such as *Code of Ethics with Interpretive Statements* (2001), *Nursing's Social Policy Statement, Second Edition* (2003), and *Nursing: Scope and Standards of Practice* (2004), as well as other specialty scope and standards, served as primary resources to the inform the workgroup's discussion and thinking. They distributed early draft language of the standards to attendees of the 2005 AALNC Annual Meeting and solicited public comments that in turn prompted further revisions.

AALNC members, specialty nursing organizations, ANA's constituent member associations, and other stakeholders then reviewed and commented on the revised draft over a period of six weeks at ANA's www.NursingWorld.org web site. All comments and suggestions were reviewed by the workgroup in preparing the final document. Reviews by the ANA Congress on Nursing Practice and Economics, and the Committee on Nursing Practice Standards and Guidelines, culminated in the recognition of legal nursing consulting as a nursing specialty, acknowledgment of the scope of practice, approval of the standards of practice, and publication of *Legal Nurse Consulting: Scope and Standards of Practice.*

During this time the AALNC published a position statement entitled The *Specialty Practice of Legal Nurse Consulting* (2005b), which defines the specialty of legal nurse consulting as a Registered Nurse practice and stresses that legal nurse consultants must maintain an active Registered Nurse license.

STANDARDS OF LEGAL NURSE CONSULTING: STANDARDS OF PRACTICE

STANDARD 1. ASSESSMENT
The legal nurse consultant collects comprehensive data pertinent to the health case or claim.

STANDARD 2. ISSUE OR PROBLEM IDENTIFICATION (DIAGNOSIS)
The legal nurse consultant analyzes the assessment data to determine the issues in the health case or claim.

STANDARD 3. OUTCOMES IDENTIFICATION
The legal nurse consultant identifies expected outcomes for the individualized plan for a given health case or claim.

STANDARD 4. PLANNING
The legal nurse consultant develops a plan that prescribes strategies and alternatives to attain expected outcomes.

STANDARD 5. IMPLEMENTATION
The legal nurse consultant implements the identified plan.

STANDARD 5A: COORDINATION OF SERVICES
The legal nurse consultant coordinates services related to the health case or claim.

STANDARD 5B: HEALTH TEACHING AND HEALTH PROMOTION
The legal nurse consultant employs strategies to promote a better understanding of health and safety related to a health case or claim.

STANDARD 5C: CONSULTATION
The legal nurse consultant provides consultation regarding a health case or claim to influence the identified plan, enhance and support the contribution of others, and effect change.

STANDARD 6. EVALUATION
The legal nurse consultant evaluates progress towards attainment of outcomes.

Standards of Legal Nurse Consulting: Standards of Professional Performance

Standard 7. Quality of Practice
The legal nurse consultant systematically enhances the quality and effectiveness of nursing practice.

Standard 8. Education
The legal nurse consultant attains knowledge and competency that reflect current nursing practice.

Standard 9. Professional Practice Evaluation
The legal nurse consultant evaluates one's own nursing practice in relation to professional practice standards and guidelines, relevant statutes, rules, and regulations.

Standard 10. Collegiality
The legal nurse consultant interacts with and contributes to the professional development of peers and colleagues.

Standard 11. Collaboration
The legal nurse consultant collaborates with clients and others in the conduct of legal nurse consulting practice.

Standard 12. Ethics
The legal nurse consultant integrates ethical provisions in all areas of practice.

Standard 13. Research
The legal nurse consultant integrates research findings into practice.

Standard 14. Resource Utilization
The legal nurse consultant considers factors related to safety, effectiveness, cost, and impact on practice in the planning and evaluation of the health case or claim.

Standard 15. Leadership
The legal nurse consultant provides leadership in the professional practice setting and the profession.

Scope of Legal Nurse Consulting Practice

Definition of Legal Nurse Consulting

Legal nurse consulting is the evaluation and analysis of facts and the rendering of informed opinions related to the delivery of nursing and healthcare services and outcomes. The legal nurse consultant is a licensed registered nurse who performs a critical analysis of clinical and administrative nursing practice, healthcare facts and issues, and their outcomes for the legal profession, healthcare professions, consumers of health care and legal services, and others as appropriate. With a strong educational and experiential foundation, the legal nurse consultant is qualified to assess adherence to standards and guidelines of nursing practice.

Evolution of Legal Nurse Consulting

Registered nurses (RNs) have been recognized as consultants to attorneys on nursing and healthcare issues and have been compensated for their expertise and contributions since the early 1970s. Nurses' earliest experiences in the legal arena were as expert witnesses who reviewed cases and offered opinions and fact testimony about nursing care in nursing malpractice cases. Gradually the courts and the legal profession began to recognize that nurses, rather than physicians, should define and evaluate the standards of nursing care and nursing practice.

As nursing and medical malpractice litigation expanded during the 1980s, nurses became more interested in and educated about the legal issues in health care. During this time attorneys searched for resources to help them understand medical records, medical literature, hospital policies and procedures, and medical testimony for an increasing case load. Attorneys and the judiciary system began to value the nurse consultant's input in these areas.

Legal Nurse Consultant became a recognized title when the National Steering Committee for the American Association of Legal Nurse Consultants formally adopted this title and with the founding of the American Association of Legal Nurse Consultants (AALNC) in 1989. Ten years later AALNC published the definitive *AALNC Position Statement on the*

Role of the Legal Nurse Consultant as Distinct from the Role of the Paralegal and Legal Assistant. This clarified the distinctions between the nursing specialty practice of legal nurse consulting and the practice of the paralegal and legal assistant as defined by the American Bar Association. AALNC recognizes legal nurse consultants (LNCs) as part of the profession of nursing, not as a special category of paralegals.

By definition, paralegals and legal assistants are persons qualified by education, training, or work experience to perform specifically delegated substantive legal work for which a lawyer is responsible. Legal education is typically a requirement for paralegals. Although many legal nurse consultants have acquired knowledge of the legal system through such experiences as consulting with attorneys and attending seminars, legal education is not a prerequisite for the independent practice of legal nurse consulting. Professional nursing education and healthcare experience make LNCs unique and valuable partners in legal processes.

The role of the legal nurse consultant differs from that of a nurse attorney. Nurse attorneys have both a nursing and a law degree, have passed a state bar examination, and are licensed to practice law. Although many nurse attorneys practice in the areas of health law, product liability, and malpractice, many choose alternative practice areas because their nursing background provides a knowledge base applicable across a broad range of legal practice areas. The American Association of Nurse Attorneys (TAANA) is the professional organization that serves these registered nurses.

Practice Characteristics and Skills

The primary role of the legal nurse consultant is to assess, analyze, evaluate, and render informed opinions on the facts related to the delivery of health care and outcomes. While the practice of each legal nurse consultant varies with practice opportunities and experience levels, certain commonalities prevail. This nursing specialty practice may include but is not limited to:

- Reviewing, summarizing, and analyzing pertinent healthcare and legal documents and comparing and correlating them to the allegations.
- Evaluating the healthcare practitioner's and facility's duty to provide services and the possible breach of this duty.

- Researching and integrating applicable literature and other evidence as it relates to the healthcare facts and issues of a case or a claim.

- Interviewing witnesses and parties pertinent to the healthcare issues.

- Facilitating communications with legal professionals strategies for successful resolutions between parties involved in healthcare-related litigation and legal matters.

- Educating attorneys and others involved in the legal process regarding the healthcare facts and issues of a case or a claim.

- Assessing issues of damages and causation relative to healthcare issues in the legal process.

- Identifying, locating, evaluating, and conferring with expert witnesses.

- Participating in the drafting of healthcare-related documents for use in the legal setting, in collaboration with an attorney.

- Developing collaborative case strategies with those practicing within the legal system.

- Providing support during discovery, depositions, trial, and other legal proceedings.

Practice Environment and Settings

The legal nurse consultant practices in a variety of settings, including law firms, government offices, insurance companies, hospital risk management departments, forensic environments, and private practice as a self-employed consultant. The legal nurse consultant serves as a liaison between the legal and healthcare communities.

Legal nurse consultants provide consultation and education to legal or healthcare professionals and others in litigation related to illness or injury, including areas such as personal injury, product liability, medical malpractice, workers' compensation, toxic torts, risk management, medical professional licensure investigation, and criminal law.

Legal nurse consultants identify their *client* as the law firm, insurance company, governmental agency, or other entity requesting or hiring their services. In the context of this document and the practice of legal nurse consultants, the *patient* refers to the recipient of nursing, medical, or allied healthcare. This care may be the subject of a lawsuit. Furthermore, the patient care may have been provided at some time in the past instead of currently.

Practice Roles

The legal nurse consultant relies on knowledge of nursing, health and wellness, and healthcare delivery systems to implement the steps of the nursing process of assessment, diagnosis (problem or issue identification), outcomes identification, planning, implementation, and evaluation. For example, the legal nurse consultant may evaluate health care for deviations from the standard of care in any element of the nursing process, or follow the steps of the nursing process to examine any healthcare element of a claim.

For example, in developing questions for a client to use in a deposition, the legal nurse consultant assesses the evidence, determines what information the attorney may need from the deponent, develops a line of questioning designed to obtain additional facts, and may even be present during the deposition to evaluate the quality of responses and offer additional or modified questions to elicit further information relevant to a claim. Additionally, the legal nurse consultant role requires effective communication skills, teaching abilities, advocacy, analytical skills, and knowledge of nursing and health care in general.

The legal nurse consultant may enter a case at any point in its active continuum: helping the attorney interview a prospective client, attending a medical examination of a plaintiff, analyzing medical records, or assisting in the development of trial exhibits. The nurse may perform duties related to healthcare issues in a variety of legal practice areas, such as:

- Medical malpractice,
- Workers compensation,
- Personal injury,
- Product liability,
- Environmental hazards,

- Forensics,
- Life care planning,
- Case management,
- Compliance, or
- Regulation.

Specialization

All legal nurse consultants are expected to integrate this scope of practice and these standards in their practice. The legal nurse consultant's role is continually evolving; some may practice in specialized roles such as nurse expert witness, forensic consultant, case manager, risk manager, and insurance industry consultant.

Nurse Expert Witness

A legal nurse consultant may testify in three specific roles—fact, liability, and economic damages witness.

The *Expert Fact Witness* explains the facts of a case with regard to illness or injury, course of treatment, and impact on the client. Drawing on a healthcare background, preparation, and experience in educating clients and families, the legal nurse consultant explains the often technical and voluminous healthcare records to attorneys, judges, and juries. This legal nurse consultant serves as a reviewer and interpreter of the healthcare records rather than offering opinions on the care rendered.

The *Liability Expert Witness* presents an evidence-based opinion about what a reasonably prudent nurse would do in a given set of circumstances. This legal nurse consultant should be one who practices in the same specialty as the defendant nurse or has similar nursing experience. The foundation for evaluating the defendant's practice is the specialty practice standards and guidelines as well as the nursing process, applicable state Nurse Practice Acts, other regulatory or accreditation requirements, review of medical and related documents, deposition testimony, and the expert nurse's own knowledge and experience. Nurse liability expert witnesses are often certified in a clinical specialty. Current clinical practice is recommended and may be required by state statute.

The *Economic Damages Expert Witness* may also be known as a *Life Care Planner*. These legal nurse consultants define the expected cost of caring for an individual over a lifetime. They use nursing knowledge and experience to understand the actual and potential needs of injured or ill persons, and they create an individualized plan allocating resources for various categories of medical needs (e.g., healthcare practitioner follow-up, studies, medications, home modifications, rehabilitation). The plan is a flexible document that is evaluated and updated throughout the individual's life. A rehabilitation nursing or case management background is recommended for the life care planner.

Forensics Nurse

These legal nurse consultants use their nursing knowledge and experience, along with their forensic training, to scientifically investigate criminal activity, traumatic accidents, and death. For example, forensic nurses evaluate whether the type and extent of injuries are consistent with the mechanism of injury in the crime. They often advocate for victims of violent crime. Forensic nurses provide services to the public and the legal community.

Case Manager

Case managers typically serve catastrophically ill or injured persons. They identify resources in the community, coordinate and monitor services, and facilitate implementation of a plan of care. Case managers work with attorneys and the insurance industry as well as healthcare providers to facilitate litigation. They may work in many legal or healthcare practices such as medical malpractice, workers' compensation, personal injury, and long-term care.

Risk Manager

The risk manager seeks to reduce risks before or after a liability is identified at any level in a healthcare organization. The risk manager assesses issues contributing to potential or actual liability, creates a plan to reduce or eliminate the risks identified, and implements a mechanism of evaluation over time to ensure maintenance of desired outcomes. The risk manager may work to assure staff or hospital compliance with regulatory standards, such as those of the Joint Commission on Accreditation of Healthcare Organizations (JCAHO).

Insurance Industry Consultant

Legal nurse consultants in the insurance field rely on their knowledge of health care and multiple healthcare delivery systems. They serve as claims adjusters, case managers, and medical benefit or utilization review coordinators. These legal nurse consultants must use their assessment skills and knowledge to understand the individual's health benefits and to assist in the determination of medical necessity. Assessment, evaluation, and negotiation skills, as well as the advocacy role, are critical to maximizing services while minimizing costs.

Educational Preparation

The legal nurse consultant brings all the expertise of the professional nurse to this specialty practice. The entry level position requires completion of a basic nursing education program, licensure as a registered nurse, and five years of registered nursing practice, preferably with a significant clinical practice component. The complexity of legal nurse consulting practice dictates a working knowledge of pertinent legal issues. Preparation in specific areas, such as legal terminology, research and literature review, and technical writing, must be combined with a fundamental understanding of the law as one practices legal nurse consulting. This education is available through formal and continuing education pathways.

Formal education for legal nurse consulting is provided by universities and community colleges. Academic degrees are offered at the associate, baccalaureate, and master's degree levels in legal nurse consulting, with the likelihood that doctoral programs will be available in the near future. This doctoral level preparation will foster the development of nursing faculty whose research will continue to advance this specialty. Some legal nurse consulting education is provided by proprietary and not-for-profit schools. AALNC has developed *Legal Nurse Consulting: Principles and Practice*, a core curriculum, and recommends that it be incorporated into educational programs for this nursing specialty.

A legal nurse consultant demonstrates a lifelong commitment to learning. Such continued learning is necessary to remain knowledgeable about clinical and legal issues that affect health care, to assure advocacy for clients and employers, and to maintain licensure and specialty certification. Annual conferences, chapter and regional programs, CD-ROM materials and online courses, and the *Journal of Legal Nurse Consulting* and other publications serve as educational resources for nurses from the entry level to the most experienced in this field. Issues such as tort reform, universal health care, Medicare and Medicaid changes, and new and different healthcare delivery models pose educational challenges for the legal nurse consultant.

Certification

Certification, as defined by the American Board of Nursing Specialties (ABNS), is the formal recognition of the specialized knowledge, skills, and experience demonstrated by the achievement of standards set by a nursing specialty to promote optimal health outcomes. While state licensure provides the legal authority for an individual to practice professional nursing, voluntary certification is obtained through individual specialty nursing certifying organizations and reflects achievement of a standard beyond licensure for specialty nursing practice. Participation in the specialty's certification process demonstrates a level of professionalism and commitment, and it allows community recognition of legal nurse consultants who have achieved a higher level of expertise in their specialty.

The American Legal Nurse Consultant Certification Board (ALNCCB) is accredited by ABNS and has offered its certification examination to qualifying legal nurse consultants since 1998. ABNS accreditation signifies to the public that a certifying organization has demonstrated compliance with rigorous standards for certification. The LNCC program, to be considered for accreditation, includes a formal practice analysis of legal nurse consultants, a defined scope and standards of practice, eligibility requirements for test candidates, development and maintenance of a psychometrically sound examination administered by a professional nursing testing company, and requirements for recertification. Additionally, ABNS standards require that the LNCC certification program maintain a research-based body of knowledge, a procedure for appeals, and organizational autonomy from AALNC.

Currently the Legal Nurse Consultant Certified (LNCC®) credential is available to those LNCs who have an active RN license, at least five years experience practicing as a registered nurse, and 2,000 hours of LNC practice in the prior three years, and have passed the ALNCCB certification exam. The LNCC is the only certification in legal nurse consulting recognized by AALNC.

LNCCs recertify after the five-year term by showing evidence of continuing education in nursing and the specialty practice, or alternatively by retesting. The LNCC credential allows the public to more readily identify those legal nurse consultants who have demonstrated a high level of experience, expertise, and commitment to this specialty practice.

Ethics and Legal Nurse Consulting

The legal nurse consultant's decisions and actions are determined in an ethical manner as described by the AALNC *Code of Ethics and Conduct* (2005a). The LNC uses other available resources to help formulate ethical decisions, such as *Code of Ethics for Nurses with Interpretive Statements* (ANA 2001), the current edition of *Legal Nurse Consulting: Scope and Standards of Practice*, and the applicable state's bar association rules of professional responsibility.

The legal nurse consultant's practice affirms the values, standards, and practices of the profession of nursing.

Examples:

- The legal nurse consultant bases opinions and recommendations on the published theory and practices of the health sciences, as well as knowledge gained through clinical experience.

- The legal nurse consultant acting as an expert nurse witness provides an objective opinion, whether engaged by the defense or by the plaintiff attorney.

The legal nurse consultant maintains confidentiality commensurate with the attorney–client privilege.

Examples:

- The legal nurse consultant adheres to ethics of confidentiality by refraining from discussing any issues pertaining to the merits of a case with anyone except the client, the client's employees, or the party whom the client represents.

- The legal nurse consultant providing expert witness testimony clarifies with the client when the legal nurse consultant communications and opinions may become discoverable and prepares written reports only on the request of the client.

The legal nurse consultant practices in a nonjudgmental and non-discriminatory manner.

Examples:

- The legal nurse consultant avoids using defamatory language when writing or talking about the person in any case.

- The legal nurse consultant acting as an expert nurse witness remains objective in the analysis of the healthcare issues in a claim and does not alter testimony to satisfy the needs or goals of the client.

The legal nurse consultant evaluates all cases and clients for conflicts of interest and declines when conflicts are evident.

Examples:

- The legal nurse consultant begins the review of a hospital claim and recognizes that one of the potential defendants is a personal friend. The legal nurse consultant notifies the client, declines the case, and recommends the services of another legal nurse consultant with comparable expertise.

- The legal nurse consultant maintains accurate records of all cases reviewed. The legal nurse consultant cross-checks each new file for conflicts of interest before accepting a case.

- The legal nurse consultant has been asked to review a claim in anticipation of providing expert witness testimony. The nursing care in question was rendered at a facility that is part of the same healthcare entity employing the expert. The legal nurse consultant declines the case because it is a conflict to testify in a case involving one's employer.

The legal nurse consultant who testifies as an expert witness confines testimony to the consultant's area of expertise.

Examples:

- A legal nurse consultant is testifying as an expert witness based on experience as a head nurse in a pulmonary unit of a large teaching hospital. Prior to that experience, this LNC taught aerobics part-time. The opposing counsel asks questions about exercise, obesity, and nutrition. The LNC declines to speak about those issues from an expert point of view, as the primary purpose for testifying in this case is to establish the nursing responsibilities in observing blood gas levels in a patient with chronic obstructive pulmonary disease.

• A legal nurse consultant working in a perinatal setting is asked to review the standard of care rendered by the nurses at the delivery of a baby with severe shoulder dystocia. The attorney asks the legal nurse consultant to give an opinion as to the cause of the child's brain injury. The legal nurse consultant limits testimony to the nursing care issues and defers causation issues to the medical practice expert.

Trends and Issues

The practice of legal nurse consulting is subject to changes and influences in health care in general, as well as in the nursing and legal professions. The following trends and issues will enhance change and growth in professional nursing and the legal nurse consulting specialty.

Tort reform has created opportunities for legal nurse consultants to serve on screening panels to prevent frivolous malpractice lawsuits and to participate in mediation efforts for resolving cases in their clinical specialty.

Legislative and regulatory changes in some states have solidified the role of legal nurse consultants as expert witnesses, and such changes are expected to proliferate. For example, in Illinois physicians can no longer testify on the nursing standard of care in nursing malpractice cases (*Sullivan v. Edward Hosp.* 2004). In some venues, advanced practice nurses testify to causation in nursing malpractice cases.

Product liability cases involve injury resulting from a drug or medical device. Increasing numbers of cases, particularly in the area of drug products, will create more practice opportunities for legal nurse consultants on both the side of the plaintiff or the defense. Legal nurse consultants may be involved in various aspects of these cases, such as screening medical records to identify appropriateness of plaintiffs' complaints, locating medical experts, and researching and summarizing healthcare literature from relevant publications.

The adult population now lives longer and with increasingly complex medical conditions, mobility and self-care deficits, and cognitive impairments like Alzheimer's disease and dementia. Varying levels of residential care are often needed to augment the healthcare services provided to seniors. This results in an increasing need for legal nurse consultants, nurse expert witnesses, and geriatric nurse case managers in the evaluation and prevention of adverse outcomes in assisted living and long-term care settings. To understand where liability for adverse outcomes resides, if in fact there is liability, the legal nurse consultant must analyze the care provided directly to the patient, the conditions under which that care was provided, and the patient's underlying health issues. The provision of home care must also be examined, as health care for the older adult is often provided at home between hospitalizations, after rehabilitation, or before placement in a residential facility.

Nursing malpractice cases may involve increased scrutiny of staffing issues related to the nursing shortage to determine any potential impact of increased reliance on temporary, part-time, float, and agency nurses in many healthcare settings. These settings include physician offices, hospitals, and long-term care and psychiatric facilities. In addition, careful analysis of nursing department functioning and institutional compliance with regulatory and accrediting standards is necessary to identify system failures that contribute to negligence. Increased opportunities exist for:

- Nurse administrators to serve as expert witnesses,

- Risk managers to address institution-wide and systems problems, and

- Legal nurse consultants to educate legal professionals regarding the complex issues related to the use of temporary nursing personnel.

Hospitals and other healthcare institutions are required to perform audits to show that they meet outcome requirements for JCAHO, the National Committee for Quality Assurance (NCQA), and other entities. The results of these quality audits are submitted to the Centers for Medicare and Medicaid Services (CMS) and are posted on the CMS website, www.cms.hhs.gov. Many hospitals hire nurses to do these audits. Nurses are uniquely qualified to perform outcome-based studies, as the evaluation of outcomes is part of the nursing process. Eventually hospitals may be reimbursed based on such audits rather than diagnosis-related groupings (DRGs). This quality management role is evolving into a new practice area for legal nurse consultants.

The advent of advanced academic programs in this nursing specialty will produce greater opportunities for legal nurse consultants to gain experience in research and to contribute to the foundation knowledge of nursing and legal nurse consulting practice. Currently, education at the master's degree level is not commonly available for legal nurse consultants. It is expected that additional advanced academic preparation will be offered at the master's and doctoral levels in the near future.

These trends and issues represent likely influences on several areas of legal nurse consulting practice. Not all legal nurse consultant roles will be affected equally; for instance, greater role diversity will be seen in long-term care and the insurance industry. Advanced academic degree programs will stimulate more research to further promote the development and implementation of evidence-based practice guidelines. New leadership opportunities in nursing, legal, academic, and judicial settings will emerge. In addition, the validity, credibility, and enhanced value of nursing and legal nurse consulting specialty practice will be advanced through greater formal recognition by research, legislative, and regulatory bodies.

STANDARDS OF LEGAL NURSE CONSULTING PRACTICE

The practice of legal nurse consulting consists of actions that are logical, interdependent, sequential, and incorporate the nursing process as a basic problem-solving process. The steps of the nursing process are: assessment, diagnosis, outcomes identification, planning, implementation, and evaluation. Nursing diagnoses are derived from an analysis of the assessment data and represent the opinions formed by the legal nurse consultant from that analysis. This process helps determine healthcare issues important to the resolution of legal claims or cases. All of these actions require clinical experience, an educational foundation, and critical thinking.

The nursing process provides the legal nurse consultant with a framework or consistent problem-solving approach for addressing a health case or claim. This framework further gives the legal nurse consultant the skills to partner with various colleagues in the legal profession to achieve positive outcomes. The nursing process also provides the means of measuring how well standards are being met by practitioners.

The Standards of Practice describe how legal nurse consultants solve problems and manage tasks. The Standards of Professional Performance are the foundation for the professional behavior of legal nurse consultants.

STANDARDS OF PRACTICE

STANDARD 1. ASSESSMENT
The legal nurse consultant collects comprehensive data pertinent to the health case or claim.

Measurement Criteria:

The legal nurse consultant:

- Collects data in a systematic and ongoing process.

- Involves healthcare providers, environmental factors, the patient and family, and others, as appropriate, in holistic data collection.

- Prioritizes data collection activities based on the health case or claim.

- Uses appropriate evidence-based assessment techniques and instruments in collecting pertinent data.

- Uses analytical models and problem-solving tools.

- Reviews literature pertinent to the health case or claim.

- Synthesizes available data, information, and knowledge relevant to the situation to identify patterns and variances.

- Documents relevant data in a retrievable format.

STANDARD 2. ISSUE OR PROBLEM IDENTIFICATION (DIAGNOSIS)

The legal nurse consultant analyzes the assessment data to determine the issues in the health case or claim.

Measurement Criteria:

The legal nurse consultant:

- Evaluates assessment data to identify issues such as:
  - Is the set of medical records complete?
  - Is the incident sufficiently substantive for a potential lawsuit or claim?
  - Should the incident undergo both physician and nurse peer review processes?
  - Is the case a high priority due to seriousness of the charge?
- Validates the issues with the client, healthcare providers, patient, and family, when possible and appropriate.
- Systematically compares and contrasts clinical findings with normal and abnormal variations and developmental events in formulating a case analysis.
- Utilizes data and information obtained during various types of interviews and reviews of records in formulating a case analysis.
- Documents issues in a manner that facilitates the determination of the expected outcomes and plan.

STANDARD 3. OUTCOMES IDENTIFICATION
The legal nurse consultant identifies expected outcomes for the individualized plan for a given health case or claim.

Measurement Criteria:

The legal nurse consultant:

- Involves the patient, family, members of the legal profession, and other healthcare providers in formulating expected outcomes, when possible and appropriate.

- Derives expected outcomes from the identified issues or problems.

- Considers associated risks, benefits, costs, current scientific evidence, and clinical expertise when formulating expected outcomes.

- Defines expected outcomes with respect for cultural diversity.

- Includes a time estimate for attainment of expected outcomes.

- Documents expected outcomes as measurable goals.

STANDARD 4. PLANNING
The legal nurse consultant develops a plan that prescribes strategies and alternatives to attain expected outcomes.

Measurement Criteria:

The legal nurse consultant:

- Develops an individualized plan, considering specific characteristics of the health case or claim (e.g., age- and culturally appropriate, environmentally sensitive).

- Develops the plan in conjunction with members of the legal profession, the patient, family, and others, as appropriate.

- Includes strategies in the plan that address each of the identified issues.

- Provides for continuity in the plan.

- Incorporates an implementation pathway or time line in the plan.

- Establishes the plan priorities.

- Utilizes the plan to provide direction to other members of the involved team.

- Defines the plan to reflect applicable statutes, rules and regulations, and standards.

- Integrates current trends and research affecting care in the planning process.

- Considers the economic impact of the plan.

- Uses standardized language or recognized terminology to document the plan.

STANDARD 5. IMPLEMENTATION
The legal nurse consultant implements the identified plan.

Measurement Criteria:

The legal nurse consultant:

- Implements the plan in a reasonable and timely manner.
- Documents implementation and any modifications, including changes in or omissions from the plan.
- Utilizes new knowledge and evidence-based strategies, where available, specific to the health case or claim.
- Utilizes resources and systems to implement the plan.
- Collaborates with colleagues and others to implement the plan.

STANDARD 5A: COORDINATION OF SERVICES
The legal nurse consultant coordinates services related to the health case or claim.

Measurement Criteria:

The legal nurse consultant:

- Coordinates implementation of the plan, such as coordinating the facts from the medical record, deposition testimony, and discussion with the experts to develop effective demonstrative evidence to be used at trial.

- Synthesizes data and information to prescribe necessary system and community support measures, such as the case manager who advocates for the patient to ensure home modifications that will increase functionality.

- Documents the coordination of the work products which make up the plan. The legal nurse consultant may:

  - Coordinate communication between the healthcare provider, patient, and family to prevent a lawsuit from being filed.

  - Advocate for care based on the cost–benefit ratio as well as the applicable state worker's compensation law.

  - Draft medical elements of a claim to be used by the attorney in various legal documents such as the complaint, demand letter, or deposition questions.

STANDARD 5B: HEALTH TEACHING AND HEALTH PROMOTION

The legal nurse consultant employs strategies to promote a better understanding of health and safety related to a health case or claim.

Measurement Criteria:

The legal nurse consultant:

- Evaluates the health and safety issues involved in a health case or claim.

- Provides health teaching related to the impact of the illness or injury on a health case or claim.

- Evaluates health information resources, such as the Internet, in the area of practice for accuracy, readability, and comprehensibility to help clients access quality health information.

- Uses health teaching methods appropriate to the health case or claim.

- Seeks opportunities for feedback and evaluation of the effectiveness of the strategies used.

STANDARD 5C: CONSULTATION

The legal nurse consultant provides consultation regarding a health case or claim to influence the identified plan, enhance and support the contribution of others, and effect change.

Measurement Criteria:

The legal nurse consultant:

- Synthesizes data, information, research, and evidence on a health case or claim when providing consultation.

- Facilitates the effectiveness of a consultation by involving the client and others, as appropriate, in decision-making and negotiating role responsibilities.

- Communicates consultation recommendations that facilitate change. For example, the LNC may provide information learned through discussions with potential experts that could influence the attorney's decision to pursue or not pursue a claim or case.

STANDARD 6. EVALUATION

The legal nurse consultant evaluates progress towards attainment of outcomes.

Measurement Criteria:

The legal nurse consultant:

- Conducts a systematic, ongoing, and criterion-based evaluation of the outcomes in relation to the structures and processes prescribed by the plan and the indicated time line.

- Includes the client and others involved in the health case or claim in the evaluative process.

- Evaluates the effectiveness of the planned strategies in relation to patient responses and the attainment of the expected outcomes.

- Documents the results of the evaluation.

- Uses ongoing assessment data to revise the diagnoses, outcomes, the plan, and the implementation as needed.

- Disseminates the results to the client and others involved in the health case or claim, as appropriate, in accordance with state and federal laws and regulations.

Standards of Professional Performance

Standard 7. Quality of Practice
The legal nurse consultant systematically enhances the quality and effectiveness of nursing practice.

Measurement Criteria:

The legal nurse consultant:

- Demonstrates quality by documenting the application of the nursing process in a responsible, accountable, and ethical manner.

- Uses the results of quality improvement activities to initiate changes in nursing practice and in the healthcare delivery system.

- Uses creativity and innovation in nursing practice to improve the delivery of legal nurse consulting services.

- Incorporates new knowledge to initiate changes in nursing practice if desired outcomes are not achieved.

- Participates in activities that improve quality of practice, such as:

  - Identifying aspects of practice important for quality monitoring.

  - Using indicators developed to monitor quality and effectiveness of nursing practice.

  - Collecting data to monitor quality and effectiveness of nursing practice.

  - Analyzing quality data to identify opportunities for improving nursing practice.

  - Formulating recommendations to improve nursing practice or outcomes.

  - Implementing activities to enhance the quality of nursing practice.

  - Developing, implementing, and evaluating policies, procedures, and guidelines to improve the quality of practice.

  - Participating on interdisciplinary teams to evaluate clinical care or health services.

Continued ▶

- Participating in efforts to minimize costs and unnecessary duplication.

- Analyzing factors related to safety, satisfaction, effectiveness, and cost–benefit options.

- Implementing processes to remove or decrease barriers in organizational systems.

STANDARD 8. EDUCATION
The legal nurse consultant attains knowledge and competency that reflect current nursing practice.

Measurement Criteria:

The legal nurse consultant:

- Participates in ongoing educational activities related to appropriate knowledge bases and professional issues.

- Demonstrates a commitment to lifelong learning through self-reflection and inquiry to identify learning needs.

- Seeks experiences that reflect current practice in order to maintain skills and competence in clinical practice or role performance.

- Acquires knowledge and skills appropriate to the specialty area, practice setting, role, or situation.

- Maintains professional records that provide evidence of competency and lifelong learning.

- Seeks experiences and formal and independent learning activities to develop and maintain clinical and professional skills and knowledge.

- Acquires and maintains professional certification, as available, in the areas of expertise, such as clinical specialty nursing practice certification and that of the Legal Nurse Consultant Certified (LNCC).

STANDARD 9. PROFESSIONAL PRACTICE EVALUATION
The legal nurse consultant evaluates one's own nursing practice in relation to professional practice standards and guidelines, relevant statutes, rules, and regulations.

Measurement Criteria:

The legal nurse consultant's practice reflects the application of knowledge of current practice standards, guidelines, statutes, rules, and regulations.

The legal nurse consultant:

- Provides services in a culturally and ethnically sensitive manner.
- Engages in self-evaluation of practice on a regular basis, identifying areas of strength as well as areas in which professional development would be beneficial. For example, the LNC may:
  - Meet on a regular basis with the employer or senior legal nurse consultant for performance appraisal when employed by a law firm.
  - Review and reflect on personal performance and plans to attend continuing education for self-improvement.
  - Establish a mentoring relationship with another legal nurse consultant who works in a similar setting, to assist in performance evaluation.
  - Conduct an annual survey of clients to determine how well the work product and selected experts met the goals of the client.
- Seeks feedback regarding one's own practice from peers, professional colleagues, clients, and others.
- Participates in systematic peer review, as appropriate. For example, the LNC may:
  - Volunteer to be a member of the quality assurance team for a national insurance company evaluating the work of in-house adjusters.
  - Establish a review board of attorneys and legal nurse consultants to review the business plan, progress of the business, and the goals and direction for future practice when in independent practice.

- Takes action to achieve goals identified during the evaluation process. For example, the LNC may:

  - Revise the format used to submit summary reports so that conclusions are more easily identified.

  - Develop a reporting template to elaborate on the potential complications and the associated expenses in the life care plan.

- Provides rationale for practice beliefs, decisions, and actions as part of the informal and formal evaluation processes, such as explaining why a particular expert or exhibit will more effectively explain the issues of a case or claim.

STANDARD 10. COLLEGIALITY

The legal nurse consultant interacts with and contributes to the professional development of peers and colleagues.

Measurement Criteria:

The legal nurse consultant:

- Shares knowledge and skills with peers and colleagues as evidenced by such activities as participating in case conferences or presentations at formal or informal meetings, presenting an educational program at a local or national AALNC conference, or submitting an article to a professional journal.

- Provides peers with feedback regarding their practice or role performance, such as answering questions posed by a subcontracting legal nurse consultant regarding the clarity and accuracy of a work product.

- Maintains professional, collegial relationships.

- Contributes to an environment conducive to the education of nurses entering the field of legal nurse consulting.

- Contributes to an environment that is conducive to the education of peers and colleagues, attorneys, patients and families, jurors, and others.

- Mentors other legal nurse consultants and colleagues, as appropriate.

- Contributes to a supportive and healthy work environment.

STANDARD 11. COLLABORATION
The legal nurse consultant collaborates with clients and others in the conduct of legal nurse consulting practice.

Measurement Criteria:

The legal nurse consultant:

- Communicates with members of the legal profession, healthcare providers, patients, and families, as appropriate, regarding the health case or claim.

- Collaborates with others in creating a documented plan focused on outcomes and decisions related to care and delivery of services.

- Partners with others to effect change and generate positive outcomes through knowledge of the patient or situation.

- Documents communications and referrals as appropriate.

STANDARD 12. ETHICS

The legal nurse consultant integrates ethical provisions in all areas of practice.

Measurement Criteria:

The legal nurse consultant:

- Uses *Code of Ethics for Nurses with Interpretive Statements* (ANA 2001) and AALNC's *Code of Ethics and Conduct* (2005a) to guide practice.

- Serves as an advocate for promoting professional standards of practice.

- Maintains confidentiality within legal and regulatory parameters.

- Maintains a professional relationship in the healthcare and legal environments.

- Demonstrates a commitment to practicing self-care, managing stress, and connecting with self and others.

- Contributes to resolving ethical issues of patients, colleagues, or systems as evidenced by such activities as participating on ethics committees.

- Reports illegal, incompetent, or impaired practice.

- Participates on multidisciplinary and interdisciplinary teams that address ethical risks, benefits, and outcomes.

STANDARD 13. RESEARCH
The legal nurse consultant integrates research findings into practice.

Measurement Criteria:

The legal nurse consultant:

- Uses the best available evidence to critically analyze, interpret, and apply research to guide decisions about the health case or claim.

- Actively participates in research activities. Such activities may include:

  - Participating on a formal research committee or program.

  - Sharing research activities and findings with peers and others.

  - Using research findings to evaluate the appropriateness of policies, procedures, and standards of practice as applied to the health case or claim.

STANDARD 14. RESOURCE UTILIZATION

The legal nurse consultant considers factors related to safety, effectiveness, cost, and impact on practice in the planning and evaluation of the health case or claim.

Measurement Criteria:

The legal nurse consultant:

- Evaluates factors such as safety, effectiveness, availability, cost and benefits, efficiency, and impact on practice, when assessing practice options that would result in the same expected outcome.

- Assigns or delegates tasks based on the health case or claim, as appropriate.

- Assists the public in becoming informed consumers about the options, costs, risks, and benefits of treatment and care, as appropriate.

STANDARD 15. LEADERSHIP

The legal nurse consultant provides leadership in the professional practice setting and the profession.

Measurement Criteria:

The legal nurse consultant:

- Provides leadership to the profession through diligent practice in a nontraditional nursing role.

- Engages in teamwork as a team player and a team builder.

- Works to create and maintain healthy work environments in local, regional, national, or international communities.

- Displays the ability to define a clear vision, associated goals, and a plan to implement and measure progress.

- Demonstrates a commitment to continuous, lifelong learning for self and others.

- Teaches others to succeed by mentoring and other strategies.

- Exhibits creativity and flexibility through times of change.

- Demonstrates energy, excitement, and a passion for quality work.

- Directs the coordination of care across settings and among care-givers, including oversight of licensed and unlicensed personnel in any assigned or delegated tasks, as appropriate.

- Serves in key roles in the work setting by participating on commit-tees, councils, and administrative teams.

- Promotes advancement of the profession through participation in professional organizations.

- Works to influence decision-making bodies to improve patient care.

- Provides direction to enhance the effectiveness of the healthcare team, as appropriate.

Glossary

Assessment. For the legal nurse consultant, the collection of data to support the systematic analysis of healthcare issues related to a health case or a claim. The first step of the nursing process, in which data are gathered and examined in preparation for the second step—diagnosis.

Client. The entity requesting or hiring the services of the legal nurse consultant. The client is typically a law firm, insurance company, governmental agency, etc. Legal nurse consultants do not work directly for the *patient*, but on behalf of the patient through the client as an intermediary.

Defendant. The person or entity against which a lawsuit is brought.

Diagnosis. The second step of the nursing process, in which data are analyzed for the purpose of identifying and describing the actual and potential health problems or the issues inherent in a health case or claim.

Duty. An action or observation that is expected to occur once a relationship has been established between two entities, such as between healthcare provider and patient.

Evaluation. The sixth step of the nursing process, in which each of the previous steps is analyzed to identify factors that enhanced or hindered progress, then modifying or terminating the plan, as necessary.

Expert fact witness. One who by virtue of special knowledge, skill, training, or experience is qualified to provide testimony to aid the fact finder in matters that exceed the common knowledge of ordinary people, but who does not offer opinions on the standard of care.

Expert witness. A witness who by virtue of special knowledge, skill, training, or experience is qualified to provide testimony to aid the fact finder in matters that exceed the common knowledge of ordinary people.

Health case or claim. The healthcare facts related to an actual or potential event, incident, or series of incidents that are the focus of legal nurse consulting practice.

Implementation. The fifth step of the nursing process, involving completion or realization of the plan of action.

Litigation. A lawsuit, legal action; includes all proceedings therein. A contest in a court of law for the purpose of enforcing a right or seeking a remedy. A judicial contest, a judicial controversy, a suit at law.

Malpractice. Misconduct, negligence, or failure to properly perform duties according to professional standards of care.

Mediation. A problem-solving process involving a neutral third party who facilitates the parties in reaching a resolution but lacks authority to render a decision.

Negligence. A failure to act as an ordinary prudent person or "reasonable man" would do under similar circumstances. There are four elements of negligence that must be proven in order for there to be a viable medical malpractice claim:

- A duty must be owed to the patient. The duty usually occurs when the healthcare provider accepts responsibility for the care and treatment of the patient.

- The breach of duty or standard of care by the professional. The standard of care for that type of specialty and that particular type of treatment must be determined to see if there has been an act of omission or commission that has caused damage to the patient.

- Proximate cause or causal connection must be evident between the breach of duty and the harm or damages that have occurred to the patient/plaintiff.

- Damages or injuries suffered by the plaintiff. Damages or injuries can take the form of any of the following, including but not limited to loss of love and affection; loss of nurturance: pain and suffering; mental anguish; emotional distress; loss of chance of survival; disfigurement; past, present, and future medical expenses; past, present, and future loss of wages; premature death; and loss of enjoyment of life.

Outcomes. Measurable, expected, and defined goals.

Outcomes Identification. The third step in the nursing process, the identification of desired activities related to the healthcare issues of a case or claim.

Patient. In the context of this document, the *patient* refers to the recipient of nursing, medical, or allied health care. This care may be the subject of a lawsuit.

Plan. A comprehensive outline of services to be delivered to meet the expected outcomes.

Plaintiff. A person who brings a legal action; the person who complains or sues a civil action and is so named in the record. A person who seeks remedial relief for an injury to rights; a complainant.

Standard. An authoritative statement enunciated and promulgated by the profession, by which the quality of practice, service, or education can be judged.

Standard of care. The degree of care that a reasonably prudent person should exercise under the same or similar circumstances. In the case of a professional (e.g., nurse, physician, lawyer), it is the degree of care that a reasonably prudent person in that profession should exercise under the same or similar circumstances.

Tort. A civil wrong or injury other than breach of contract.

Toxic tort. A civil wrong arising from exposure to a toxic substance such as asbestos, radiation, or hazardous waste. A toxic tort can be remedied by a civil lawsuit (usually a class action) or by administrative action.

REFERENCES

American Association of Legal Nurse Consultants (AALNC). 1999. *Position statement on the role of the legal nurse consultant as distinct from the role of the paralegal and legal assistant.* http://www.aalnc.org/hire/roll.cfm

———. 2003. *Legal nurse consulting: Principles and practice.* 2nd edition. (Patricia W. Iyer, editor) Boca Raton, FL: CRC Press.

———. 2005a. *Code of ethics and conduct of the American Association of Legal Nurse Consultants.* http://www.aalnc.org/about/whatis.cfm

———. 2005b. *Position statement: the specialty practice of legal nurse consulting 2005.* http://www.aalnc.org/about/position.cfm

American Nurses Association (ANA). 2001. *Code of ethics for nurses with interpretive statements.* Washington, DC: American Nurses Publishing.

———. 2003. *Nursing's social policy statement.* 2nd edition. Washington, DC: Nursesbooks.org.

———. 2004. *Nursing: Scope and standards of practice.* Washington, DC: Nursesbooks.org.

Sullivan v. Edward Hosp., 209 Ill. 2d 100 (Ill. 2004).
Available online:
    http://www.state.il.us/court/OPINIONS/SupremeCourt/2004/February/Opinions/Html/95409.htm

Illinois Supreme Court summary (filed February 5, 2004) available online:
    http://www.state.il.us/court/OPINIONS/SupremeCourt/2004/February/Summaries/Html/95409s.htm

Index

A

Advocacy, 4, 6, 7
  coordination of services and, 21
  ethics and, 32
Age-appropriate care. *See* Cultural
    competence
American Association of Legal Nurse
    Consultants (AALNC), *vii–viii*, 1–2,
    7–8
  Code of Ethics and Conduct, 9, 32
  collegiality and, 30
  position statement on legal nurse
    consulting, 1–2
American Association of Nurse Attorneys
    (TAANA), 2
American Bar Association, 2
American Board of Nursing Specialties
    (ABNS), 8
American Legal Nurse Consultant
    Certification Board (ALNCCB), 8
  See also Certification and
    credentialing
American Nurses Association (ANA), *vii*, *viii*
  Code of Ethics for Nurses with
    Interpretive Statements, *vii*, 9, 32
  Nursing: Scope and Standards of
    Practice, *vii*
  Nursing's Social Policy Statement, *vii*
  Standards of Nursing Practice, *vii*
Analysis. *See* Critical thinking, analysis,
    and synthesis
Assessment, 2, 3, 7
  defined, 37
  evaluation and, 24
  issue or problem identification and, 17
  standard of practice, 16
  step in nursing process, *vii*, 4, 15, 37
Assisted living, 12
Attorneys
  collegiality and, 30
  consultation and, 23
  coordination of services and, 21
  legal nurse consultants and, 2, 3, 4, 6,
    9, 11

nurse attorney, 2
outcomes identification and, 18
planning and, 19
professional practice evaluation and,
    28
registered nurses and, 1

B

Body of knowledge, 4, 5
  ethics, 9
  education and, 27
  forensics, 6
  implementation and, 20
  insurance industry, 7
  outcomes identification and, 18
  professional practice evaluation and,
    28
  quality of practice and, 25

C

Care recipient. *See* Patient
Care standards. *See* Standards of practice
Case management, 5, 6, 7, 12
  See also Coordination of services
Centers for Medicare and Medicaid
    Services (CMS), 12
Certification and credentialing, *viii*, 1, 3,
    5, 8–9, 12
  education and, 7, 27
  leadership and, 35
  nurse attorneys, 2
Client
  advocacy, 7
  consultation and, 23
  defined, 3–4, 37
  ethics and, 9, 10
  evaluation and, 24
  health teaching and health
    promotion and, 22
  issue or problem identification and,
    17
  professional practice evaluation and,
    28
  See also Patient

Clinical settings. *See* Practice settings
Code of Ethics and Conduct, 9
Code of Ethics for Nurses with Interpretive Statements, *vii*, 9, 32
  See also Ethics
Collaboration, 3, 15
  consultation and, 23
  implementation and, 20
  standard of professional performance, 31
  See also Healthcare providers; Interdisciplinary health care
Collegiality, 15
  consultation and, 23
  ethics and, 32
  implementation and, 20
  planning and, 19
  professional practice evaluation and, 28
  research and, 33
  standard of professional performance, 30
Communication, 3, 4
  collaboration and, 31
  consultation and, 23
  coordination of services and, 21
  evaluation and, 24
  leadership and, 35
  research and, 33
  resource utilization and, 34
Competence assessment. *See* Certification and credentialing
Compliance, 5, 6, 8, 12
Confidentiality, 9, 32
  See also Ethics
Conflict of interest, 10
  See also Ethics
Consultation
  standard of practice, 23
Continuity of care, 19
Coordination of services
  leadership and, 35
  standard of practice, 21
  See also Case management; Interdisciplinary health care
Cost control, 6, 7
  coordination of services and, 21

outcomes identification and, 18
planning and, 19
quality of practice and, 26
resource utilization and, 34
Cost-effectiveness. *See* Cost control
Credentialing. *See* Certification and credentialing
Criminal law, 3, 6
Criteria
  assessment, 16
  collaboration, 31
  collegiality, 30
  consultation, 23
  coordination of services, 21
  education, 27
  ethics, 32
  evaluation, 24
  health teaching and health promotion, 22
  implementation, 20
  issue or problem identification, 17
  leadership, 35
  outcomes identification, 18
  planning, 19
  professional practice evaluation, 28–29
  quality of practice, 25–26
  research, 33
  resource utilization, 34
Critical thinking, analysis, and synthesis, 1, 2, 4, 15
  assessment and, 16
  consultation and, 23
  coordination of services and, 21
  evaluation and, 24
  issue or problem identification and, 17
  nursing process and, *vii*
  planning and, 19
  quality of practice and, 25
  research and, 33
Cultural competence
  ethics and, 10
  outcomes identification and, 18
  planning and, 19
  professional practice evaluation and, 28

D

Data collection
  assessment and, 16
  quality of practice and, 25
Decision-making
  collaboration and, 31
  consultation and, 23
  leadership and, 35
  professional practice evaluation and, 28
Defendant, 5
  defined, 37
Depositions, 3, 4, 5
  coordination of services and, 21
Diagnosis
  defined, 37
  step in nursing process, *vii*, 4, 15, 37
  See also Issue or problem identification
Diagnosis-related groupings (DRGs), 12–13
Discovery, 3, 10
Documentation, 3, 5
  assessment and, 16
  collaboration and, 31
  coordination of services and, 21
  education and, 27
  ethics and, 10
  evaluation and, 24
  implementation and, 20
  issue or problem identification and, 17
  outcomes identification and, 18
  planning and, 19
  professional practice evaluation and, 29
  quality of practice and, 25
Duty (defined), 37

E

Economic damage expert witness, 6
  See also Life care planner
Economic issues. *See* Cost control
Education of attorneys, 3, 4, 5, 12
Education of legal nurse consultants, 1, 2, 7–8, 13, 15
  collegiality and, 30
  credentialing and, 9
  leadership and, 35

standard of professional performance, 27
  See also Mentoring; Professional development
Education of patients and families, 5
  See also Family; Health teaching and health promotion; Patient
Environment. *See* Practice environment
Environmental factors and hazards, 4, 16
  See also Toxic torts
Ethics, 9–11
  quality of practice and, 25
  standard of professional performance, 32
  See also Code of Ethics for Nurses with Interpretive Statements; Laws, statutes, and regulations
Evaluation, 6, 7
  defined, 37
  health teaching and health promotion, 22
  resource utilization and, 34
  standard of practice, 24
  step in nursing process, *vii*, 4, 12, 15, 37
Evidence-based practice, 5, 13
  assessment and, 16
  consultation and, 23
  implementation and, 20
  outcomes identification and, 18
  See also Research
Expert fact witness, 5
  defined, 37
Expert witness, 1, 2, 5–6, 11, 12
  defined, 37
  ethics and, 9–11
  See also Witness

F

Family
  assessment and, 16
  collaboration and, 31
  collegiality and, 30
  coordination of services and, 21
  issue or problem identification and, 17
  outcomes identification and, 18
  planning and, 19
  See also Education of patients and families; Patient

Financial issues. *See* Cost control
Forensics nurses, 5, 6

G
Guidelines. *See* Standards of practice;
  Standards of professional
  performance

H
Health case or claim (defined), 37
Health law, 2
Health teaching and health promotion
  standard of practice, 22
Healthcare delivery, 4, 8
  quality of practice and, 25
Healthcare providers
  assessment and, 16
  case management and, 6
  collaboration and, 31
  coordination of services and, 21
  insurance consulting and, 7
  issue or problem identification and,
    17
  outcomes identification and, 18
  See also Collaboration;
    Interdisciplinary health care
Healthcare team. *See* Collaboration;
  Interdisciplinary health care
Home care, 12
Human resources. *See* Professional
  development

I
Implementation
  case management and, 6
  coordination of services and, 21
  defined, 37
  evaluation and, 24
  leadership and, 35
  planning and, 19
  quality of practice and, 25, 26
  standard of practice, 20
  step in nursing process, *vii*, 4, 15, 37
Information. *See* Data collection
Insurance industry, 6, 13
Insurance industry consultant, 7

Interdisciplinary health care
  ethics and, 32
  leadership and, 35
  quality of practice and, 25
  See also Collaboration; Healthcare
    providers
Internet, 22
Issue or problem identification
  standard of practice, 17
  See also Diagnosis

J
Joint Commission on Accreditation of
  Healthcare Organizations (JCAHO),
  6, 12
Journal of Legal Nurse Consulting, 8
Judges, 5
Juries, 5, 30

K
Knowledge base. *See* Body of knowledge

L
Laws, statutes, and regulations, 5, 6, 11, 12,
  13
  ethics and, 9
  evaluation and, 24
  planning and, 19
  professional practice evaluation and,
    28
  See also Ethics
Lawyers. See Attorneys
Leadership, 13
  standard of professional
    performance, 35
Legal assistants, 2
Legal Nurse Consultant Certified (LNCC),
  8–9, 27
  See also Certification and
    credentialing
Legal nurse consulting, 1–13
  attorneys and, 2, 3, 4, 6, 9, 11
  body of knowledge, 4, 5, 6, 7, 9
  certification, *viii*, 1, 2, 3, 5, 7, 8–9, 12, 27,
    35
  characteristics, 2–3

Personal injury, 3, 4, 6
Plan (defined), 39
Planning
    collaboration and, 31
    consultation and, 23
    defined, 39
    evaluation and, 24
    implementation and, 20
    issue or problem identification and, 17
    leadership and, 35
    outcomes identification and, 18
    resource utilization and, 34
    standard of practice, 19
    step in nursing process, *vii*, 4, 15, 37
    See also Life care planning
Policy. *See* Healthcare policy
Position statements, *viii*, 1
Practice environment, 3–4, 12
    assessment and, 16
    collegiality and, 30
    education and, 27
    leadership and, 35
    planning and, 19
Practice roles. *See* Roles in legal nurse
    consulting practice
Practice settings. *See* Practice
    environment
Preceptors. *See* Mentoring
Privacy. *See* Confidentiality
Process. *See* Nursing process
Product liability, 2, 3, 4, 11
Professional development
    collegiality and, 30
    education and, 27
    professional practice evaluation and,
    28
    See also Education; Leadership
Professional organizations, *vii*, *viii*, 35
    See also American Association of
    Legal Nurse Consultants; American
    Nurses Association
Professional performance. *See* Standards
    of professional performance
Professional practice evaluation
    collegiality and, 30
    standard of professional performance,
    28–29

Q
Quality of practice
    standard of professional performance,
    25–26

R
Recipient of care. *See* Patient
Referrals. *See* Collaboration;
    Coordination of services
Registered nursing, 1, 8
Regulatory issues. *See* Laws, statutes,
    and regulations
Research, 3, 11, 13
    assessment and, 16
    consultation and, 23
    coordination of services and, 21
    education and, 7
    planning and, 19
    standard of professional
    performance, 33
    See also Evidence-based practice
Resource utilization
    case management and, 6
    health teaching and health
    promotion, 22
    implementation and, 20
    insurance consulting and, 7
    standard of professional
    performance, 34
Risk assessment, 3, 5, 6, 12
    ethics and, 32
    outcomes identification and, 18
    resource utilization and, 34
Roles in legal nurse consulting practice,
    4–7, 13
    education and, 27

S
Safety assurance
    health teaching and health
    promotion, 22
    quality of practice and, 26
    resource utilization and, 34
Scientific findings. *See* Evidence-based
    practice; Research
Scope of practice, 1–13
Self care and self-management, 12, 32

Senior health care, 12
Settings. *See* Practice environment
Significant others. *See* Family
Specialty certification, 8, 9
   See also Certification and
      credentialing
Specialty practice, *vii, viii,* 5–7
   education and, 27
Standard (defined), 39
Standards of care,
   defined, 39
   origins, *vii–viii*
   See also Standards of practice
Standards of practice, *ix,* 8, 15, 16–24
   assessment, 16
   consultation, 23
   coordination of services, 21
   evaluation, 24
   health teaching and health
      promotion, 22
   implementation, 20
   issue or problem identification, 17
   nursing process as framework for, 15
   outcomes identification, 18
   planning, 19
Standards of professional performance,
      x, 15, 25–35
   collaboration, 31
   collegiality, 30
   education, 27

ethics, 32
leadership, 35
professional practice evaluation, 28–29
quality of practice, 25–26
research, 33
resource utilization, 34
Synthesis. *See* Critical thinking, analysis,
      and synthesis

T
Teaching. *See* Education; Health
      teaching and health promotion
Teams and teamwork. *See*
      Interdisciplinary health care
Terminology, 7, 19, 37–39
Tort (defined), 39
Tort reform, 8, 11
Toxic torts, 3
   defined, 39
   See also Environmental hazards
Trends in legal nurse consulting, 11–13
Trials, 3, 4, 21

W
Witness, 3
   See also Expert witness
Work environment. *See* Practice
      environment
Worker's compensation, 3, 4, 6
   coordination of services and, 21